WHY IS A COLONEL CALLED A "KERNAL"? THE ORIGIN OF AMERICAN RANKS AND INSIGNIA

WHY IS A COLONEL CALLED A "KERNAL"?
The Origin of American Ranks and Insignia

by

Raymond Oliver

Fireship Press
www.FireshipPress.com

ISBN-13: 978-1-934757-59-8
ISBN-10: 1-934757-59-4

BISAC Subject Headings:
    HIS027110   HISTORY / Military / United States
    HIS027000   HISTORY / Military / General

This work is based on the paper by Raymond Oliver, Museum Curator for McClellan Aviation Museum entitled *Why is the Colonel Called "Kernal"? The Origin of the Ranks and Rank Insignia Now Used by the United States Armed Forces* Published by the Office of History, Sacramento Air Logistics Center, McClellan AFB CA, August, 1983

Address all correspondence to:
Fireship Press, LLC
P.O. Box 68412
Tucson, AZ 85737

Or visit our website at:
www.FireshipPress.com

1.0

CONTENTS

PREFACE

The armed forces does not have a handy booklet explaining the origin and history of the ranks and insignia of the military. The recently established Project Warrior and the Air Force Logistics Command's Heritage Program have sparked interest in this area of military history.

Raymond Oliver, in answering a request from a colonel as to why her title was pronounced "kernal" and where her eagle insignia originated, began this booklet to trace development of general categories of ranks. Mr. Oliver produced the original booklet independently, but when requested to have it printed as a special study, eagerly cooperated. A few minor editorial changes and corrections have been made to the original draft, first published in 1982. The booklet, in the interest of space, is not footnoted but a list of sources follows the narrative.

The military, it is hoped, will have a deeper appreciation for his or her insignia and wear it proudly. Civilians unfamiliar with the rank structure of the military will find this booklet helpful in answering questions of what can be confusing to the neophyte.

MAURICE A. MILLER
Chief, Office of History
August, 1983

FOREWORD

Why is Colonel pronounced "kernal"? Why does a Lieutenant General outrank a Major General? Why is Navy Captain a higher rank than Army-Air Force-Marine Captain? Why do Sergeants wear chevrons? Was John J. Pershing a six-star General?

As I searched for answers to these and other such questions I found little easily available information on the origins and histories of the military ranks and rank insignia. I wrote this booklet to help correct that situation.

Many people helped me find this sometimes obscure information, among them Captain James Tily, USN (Retired), Detmar Finke, Colonel Richard Allen, Stanley Kalkus, John Slonaker, J. David Browne, Mary Haynes, Bob Aquilina, Opal Landen, Marjorie Whittington, Michael McAfee, A.W. Haarman, D.J. Crawford, Earl Jastram, Lynwood Carranco, Bonnie Olson, Truman Grandy, Dr. S.J. Lewis, Vern Morten, Emily Slocum, Carroll Pursell, Janet Griffith, Pat Carter and Olga Oliver.

RAYMOND OLIVER
McClellan Aviation Museum

INTRODUCTION

The U.S. military services still use many of the ranks they started with when they began in 1775 at the beginning of our Revolutionary War. The leaders adopted the organization, regulations and ranks of the British army and navy with only minor changes. This is not surprising because our Revolutionary Army was made up of colonial militia units that had been organized and drilled by British methods for many years. Most of the military experience of the soldiers and their officers, George Washington among them, had come from service in militia units fighting alongside British army units during the French and Indian War of 1754-1763.

The British navy was the most successful in the world at that time so the Continental Congress' navy committee, headed by John Adams who became President after Washington, copied it as they set up our Navy. They adopted some British regulations with hardly a change in the wording. Our first Marine units patterned themselves after British marines.

Revolutionary Army rank insignia, however, did not follow the British patterns but was similar to the insignia used by the French, our allies after 1779. After the war our Army often used the uniform styles and some insignia of the British as well as the French armies. During the latter part of the Nineteenth Century German army styles also influenced our Army's dress. Our Navy used rank insignia and uniforms similar to the British navy's during the Revolutionary War and afterwards. Marine rank insignia has usually been similar to the Army's, especially after 1840.

The Coast Guard dates from 1915 when Congress combined the Revenue Cutter Service, which started in 1790, with the U.S. Life Saving Service. During World War I Coast Guard ranks became the same as the Navy's. The Air Force started as a separate service in 1947. Its officers use the same ranks and rank insignia as the Army. I will discuss the enlisted rank insignia later.

The basic names for members of the military professions go back several centuries. A Seaman's occupation is on the sea and his name, from an Old English word that was pronounced see-man, means a person whose occupation is on the sea. A Sailor is a person professionally involved with navigation or sailing. His name, which comes from the Old English word saylor, means just that, a person professionally involved with navigation. A Marine gets his name from the Latin word *marinus*, which means something pertaining to the sea. A Soldier is a person who serves in a military force for pay. His name comes from the Latin *soldus*, a contraction of another Latin word *solidus*, a Roman coin used for, among other things, paying military men.

ENLISTED RANKS

THE ORIGIN
OF CHEVRONS

Chevron is a French word meaning rafter or roof, which is what a chevron looks like; two straight lines meeting at an angle just as do rafters. It has been an "honourable ordinarie" in heraldry since at least the Twelfth Century.

Ordinaries are simple straight line forms that seem to have originated in the wood or iron bars used to fasten together or strengthen portions of shields. Other ordinaries include the cross, the diagonal cross or "x," the triangle, the "y," and horizontal, vertical and diagonal lines. The chevron was a basic part of the colorful and complicated science of heraldry. It appeared on the shields and coats-of-arms of knights, barons and kings.

Chevrons were thus easily recognized symbols of honor. That might by why French soldiers started wearing cloth chevrons with the points up on their coat sleeves in 1777 as length of service and good conduct badges. Some British units also used them to show length of service.

In 1803 the British began using chevrons with the points down as rank insignia. Sergeants wore three and Corporals

1

two. Perhaps they wore them with the points down to avoid confusion with the earlier length of service chevrons worn with the points up. Some British units also used chevrons of gold lace as officers' rank insignia.

British and French soldiers who served in our Revolutionary War wore chevrons as did some American soldiers. In 1782 General George Washington ordered that enlisted men who had served for three years "with bravery, fidelity and good conduct" wear as a badge of honor "a narrow piece of white cloth, of angular form" on the left sleeve of the uniform coat.

In 1817 Sylvanus Thayer, the superintendent of the U.S. Military Academy, West Point, used chevrons to show cadet rank. From there they spread to the rest of the Army and Marine Corps. From 1820 to 1830 Marine Captains wore three chevrons of gold lace with points down on each sleeve above the elbows of their dress uniforms. Lieutenants wore one or two gold lace chevrons depending on whether they were staff or command officers. Marine Noncommissioned Officers started wearing cloth chevrons with the points up as rank insignia in 1836. They had been wearing them for three years as length of service badges. In 1859 they began wearing chevrons in about the same patterns they do today.

Starting in 1820 Army company grade officers and Sergeants wore one chevron with the point up on each arm. The officers' chevrons were of gold or silver lace, depending on the wearer's branch of service. Captains wore their chevrons above the elbow while Lieutenants wore theirs below.

Sergeant Majors and Quartermaster Sergeants wore worsted braid chevrons above the elbow while other Sergeants and Senior Musicians wore theirs below. Corporals wore one chevron on the right sleeve above the elbow.

By 1833 the Army and Marine company grade officers had stopped wearing chevrons and returned to epaulettes as rank insignia. Sergeants of the Army dragoons then began wearing three chevrons with points down and Corporals two. All other NCOs wore cloth epaulettes to show their rank.

From 1847 to 1851 some Army NCOs wore chevrons with the points up on their fatigue uniform jackets but still used cloth epaulettes on their dress uniforms. After 1851 all Army NCOs wore chevrons with points down until 1902 when the Army turned the points up and adopted the patterns used today, two chevrons for Corporals, three for Sergeants and combinations of arcs and other devices beneath the chevrons for higher grades of Sergeants.

The stripes worn by Air Force members date from 1948. The basic design was one of several presented to 150 NCOs at Bolling Air Force Base, Washington D.C., in late 1947 or early 1948. Some 55 percent of the NCOs preferred that design so on March 9, 1948, General Hoyt S. Vandenberg, then the Air Force Vice Chief of Staff, accepted their choice and approved the design. Naturally, it took some time to obtain and distribute the new stripes so it could have been a year or more before all Air Force members got them.

Whoever designed the stripes might have been trying to combine the shoulder patch worn by members of the Army Air Forces during World War II and the insignia used on aircraft. The patch featured wings with a pierced star in the center while the aircraft insignia was a star with two bars. The stripes might be the bars from the aircraft insignia slanted gracefully upward to suggest wings. The silver grey color contrasts with the blue uniform and might suggest clouds against blue sky.

Most enlisted service members wear chevrons or stripes to show their ranks. The exceptions are the lowest three grades of Navy and Coast Guard Seamen and the Army Specialists. The Seamen wear one, two or three diagonal stripes or "hash-marks" on their sleeves. These stripes first appeared on the cuffs of sailors' jumpers in 1886. Petty Officers and Seamen First Class wore three stripes, Seamen Second Class two stripes and Seamen Third Class one stripe. Shortly after World War II the Navy moved the stripes to its Seamen's upper arms, as did the Coast Guard.

Army Specialists wear an insignia that combines a spread eagle and, depending on the pay grade, arcs—sometimes called "bird umbrellas." The eagle and arcs are mounted on a patch that suggests inverted chevrons. The badge appeared in 1955 as part of an effort to differentiate between the Army's technical or support specialists who were not NCOs and the NCOs.

No Insignia

PRIVATE

Private comes from the Latin word *privus* or perhaps *privo* that meant an individual person and later an individual without (deprived of) an office.

The term as a military rank seems to come from the Sixteenth Century when individuals had the privilege of enlisting or making private contracts to serve as soldiers in military units. Before the Sixteenth Century many armies were simply feudal levies in which the lords forced their serfs or subjects to serve.

Airman is a recent word that means somebody involved with flying. The Air Force gave that title to the members of its four lowest enlisted ranks in 1952.

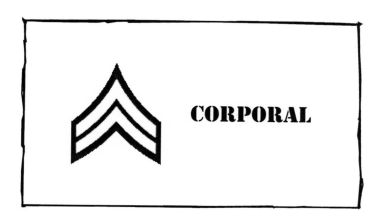

CORPORAL

Corporals often command squads in our Army and Marine Corps. That was also their job in the Fifteenth Century Italian armies.

An important tactical formation was the *squadra*, or square, headed by a reliable veteran called the *capo de'squadra* or head of the square.

The title seems to have changed to *caporale* by the Sixteenth Century and meant the leader of a small body of soldiers. About that time the French picked up the term and pronounced it in various ways, one of them being corporal, which indicates a mixing of the Latin word *corpus* or French *corps*, both of which meant body.

The British adopted corporal in the Seventeenth or Eighteenth Century and it has been a part of their army ever since. The British gave the Corporal his two stripes when they started using chevrons in 1803.

SERGEANT

The Sergeant started out as a servant, *serviens* in Latin, to a knight in medieval times. He became a fighting man probably out of self preservation, because combat in those days often amounted to cutting down everybody within reach, regardless of whether they were armed.

He became an experienced warrior who might ride a horse but was not wealthy enough to afford all the equipment and retainers to qualify as a knight. As an experienced soldier he might be called upon to take charge of a group of serfs or other common people forced to serve in an army of feudal levies. The Sergeant would conduct what training he could to teach his charges to fight, lead them into battle and, most important, keep them from running away in the process.

Sergeant was not a rank but an occupation. He might lead others he might fight alone or as a member of a group of sergeants, or he might serve the lord of his village as a policeman or guard. The modern title "sergeant-at-arms" used by many clubs recalls armed Sergeants who kept order at meetings.

WHY IS A COLONEL CALLED A "KERNAL"?

The English borrowed the word "sergeant" from the French in about the Thirteenth Century. They spelled it several different ways and pronounced it both as SARgent and SERgeant. The latter was closer to the French pronunciation. The SARgeant pronunciation became the most popular, however, so that when the Nineteenth Century dictionary writers agreed that the word should be spelled "sergeant" they could not change the popular pronunciation. Thus, we say SARgeant while the French and others say SERgeant.

Sergeant became a regular position and then a rank as army organizations evolved. It has been a key rank in British and European armies for several hundred years. When our Army and Marine Corps started in 1775 it was natural that both include Sergeants.

The rank's many duties and levels of responsibility have lead to several grades of Sergeant. The Air Force used to have six grades, while the Army and the Marines only had five. The sixth grade was a "Buck" Sergeant (E-4). Since the dual (E-4) rank of Senior Airman and Sergeant proved confusing to the other branches of service, and did not include more pay and only rarely more responsibility, the Air Force promoted its last Senior Airman to "Buck" Sergeant in May 1990 and phased the rank out over the next six years.

At present the Air Force, Army and Marines all have five grades of Sergeant ranging from (E-5) to (E-9).

PETTY OFFICER

The Petty Officer can trace his title back to the old French word petit meaning something small. Over the years the word also came to mean minor, secondary and subordinate. In medieval and later England just about every village had several "petite", "pety" or "petty" officials/officers who were subordinate to such major officials as the steward or sheriff. The petty officers were the assistants to the senior officials.

The senior officers of the early British warships, such as the Boatswain, Gunner and Carpenter, also had assistants or "mates." Since the early seamen knew "petty officers" in their home villages, they used the term to describe the minor officials aboard their ships. A ship's Captain or Master chose his own Petty Officers who served at his pleasure. At the end of a voyage or whenever the ship's crew was paid off and released, the Petty Officers lost their positions and titles. There were Petty Officers in the British navy in the Seventeenth Century and perhaps earlier, but the rank did not become official until 1808.

Petty Officers were important members of our Navy right from its beginnings and were also appointed by their ship's

Captain. They did not have uniforms or rank insignia, and they usually held their appointments only while serving on the ship whose Captain had selected them.

Petty Officers in our Navy got their first rank insignia in 1841 when they began wearing a sleeve device showing an eagle perched on an anchor. Some Petty Officers wore the device on their left arms while others wore it on their right. All wore the same device. Specialty or rating marks did not appear officially until 1866, but they seem to have been in use for several years previously. It is not uncommon for regulations to give formal status to practices that are already well established.

In 1885 the Navy recognized three classes of Petty Officers—first, second and third—and in the next year let them wear rank insignia of chevrons with the points down under a spread eagle and rating mark. The eagle faced left instead of right as it does today.

The present Petty Officer insignia came about in 1894 when the Navy established the Chief Petty Officer rank and gave him the three chevrons with arc and eagle. The first, second and third class Petty Officers also began wearing the insignia they do today.

OFFICERS

OFFICER INSIGNIA

Officers show their rank by wearing metal or embroidered insignia on their shoulders, collars, caps or sleeve cuffs. In addition, Navy and Coast Guard officers wear stripes of gold braid on their cuffs or shoulder marks, sometimes called shoulder boards. Today's insignia are fairly standard among the services and easy to recognize; but it has not always been so.

Over the years rank has been shown by such things as the number, size and pattern of buttons on their coats, sleeves or coattails; sashes worn across the chest or around the waist; the amount of gold, silver or other kinds of braid; cockades or plumes on hats; markings on saddle blankets; the cut and quality of uniform cloth; or by carrying a spontoon, a spear-like instrument that was both a weapon and a mark of authority.

In the early years of our military services the rank devices differed so much among the various Army corps and Navy units that it was difficult for service members of one activity to recognize the ranks of another activity.

EPAULETTES AND SHOULDER STRAPS

Before the Twentieth Century, epaulettes and shoulder straps were common devices to signal rank.

Epaulettes, from *epaule* an old French word for shoulder, seem to have started out as cloth straps worn on the shoulders to help keep shoulder sashes and belts in position. Another story has them beginning as pieces of armor to protect the shoulders.

By the time of our Revolutionary War epaulettes worn by British and French officers had become elaborate affairs of gold or silver that started at the collar and ended at the point of the shoulder with heavy fringes of gold or silver wire. To some they looked like fancy hair brushes. They were also very expensive being made of gold or silver, sometimes solid metal and other times plated. Epaulettes for Sergeants and other enlisted men were of cheaper metals or cloth.

In our Army officers started wearing gold or silver epaulettes in 1780 during the Revolutionary War and continued to do so until 1872, mostly on their dress uniforms. Army generals wore epaulettes until early in the Twentieth Century. Navy officers also started wearing epaulettes during the Revolutionary War and did not give them up for their full dress uniforms until just before World War II. Marine officers wore epaulettes on their special full dress uniforms until 1922.

The embroidered rank insignia usually appeared on the epaulette strap or near the "crescent," the rounded portion over the end of the shoulder. For some ranks, such as Major or Second Lieutenant, the size of the epaulette, or the size of the fringes, were the main clues of rank since those officers did not wear insignia.

Besides being expensive it seems that epaulettes made pretty good targets, so in 1831 the Army switched to shoulder straps for other than dress uniforms. The Navy had been using straps since 1830. The officers wore the straps across their shoulders at the sleeve seams of their coats.

Usually the straps had raised edges of embroidered gold or silver with the rank insignia embroidered between the edges. Navy officers wore shoulder straps until 1899 when they changed to their current shoulder marks. Army and Marine officers wore the straps until the first few years of this century when they changed to metal pin-on type insignia. They started wearing the metal insignia just before the end of the Nineteenth Century on their new khaki or olive drab uniforms, but also wore the straps with more formal attire. Army officers still wear shoulder straps on their blue uniforms. Many also wear embroidered insignia.

Navy officers started wearing stripes of gold lace on their sleeve cuffs in 1852 but in different patterns than today. Captains, for instance, had just three stripes. I will tell when each rank got its current number of stripes when I discuss that rank. The use of metal pin-on rank insignia by Navy officers started in 1941 when they wore the insignia on the collars of their khaki shirts.

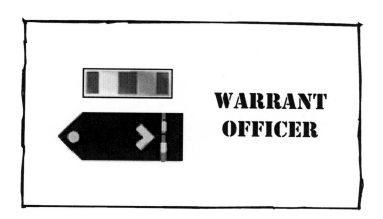

WARRANT OFFICER

The "warrant" portion of the Warrant Officer's title comes from the old French word *warant* that meant variously a protector, a defense and an authorization. It is also the source of our modern word "warranty."

In 1040 when five English ports began furnishing warships to King Edward the Confessor in exchange for certain privileges, they also furnished crews whose officers were the Master, Boatswain, Carpenter and Cook. Later these officers were "warranted" by the British Admiralty. They maintained and sailed the ships and were the standing officers of the navy.

Soldiers commanded by Captains would be on board the ships to do the fighting, but they had nothing to do with running the ships. The word "soldiering" came about as a seaman's term of contempt for the soldiers and anyone else who avoided shipboard duties.

The warranted officers were often the permanent members of the ships' companies. They stayed with the ships in port between voyages as caretakers supervising repairs and refitting. Other crewmen and soldiers might change with each voyage. Early in the Fourteenth Century the Purser joined the warrant officers. He was originally "the clerk of burser." During the following centuries the Gunner, Surgeon, Chaplain, Master-at-arms, Schoolmaster and others signed on.

Warrant Officers were members of our Navy right from its beginning. There were Warrant Officers on the ships of the Continental Navy during the Revolutionary War. When Congress created our Navy in 1794 it listed the Warrant Officers as the Sailing Masters, Purser, Boatswain, Gunner, Carpenter, Sailmaker and Midshipman.

Navy Warrant Officers began wearing blue and gold stripes in 1853—on their caps. They had stripes of half-inch wide gold lace separated by a quarter-inch wide stripe of blue cloth. In 1888 Chief Warrant Officers started wearing the sleeve stripe of a single strip of half-inch wide gold lace broken at intervals by sections of blue thread half an inch wide. In 1919 the other Navy Warrant Officers began wearing sleeve stripes of gold lace broken by sections of blue.

Our Revolutionary Army had Warrant Officers but otherwise the Army and Marines did not have them until the Twentieth Century. In 1916 the Marines made some of their Gunners and Quartermaster Clerks Warrant Officers. In 1918 Pay Clerks could also become Warrants. Also in 1918, the Army created Warrant Officers in its Mine Planter Service to serve as Masters, Mates and Engineers of its seagoing vessels.

Congress authorized more Army Warrant Officers in 1920 in clerical, administrative and musical activities, but the intent seems to have been to reward enlisted men for long service or provide positions for World War I officers who could not hold their commissions after the war. Between 1922 and 1936 the Army promoted only a few band leaders and Mine Planter Service members to warrant status. In 1936 the Army held competitive examinations to replenish its Warrant Officer eligibility lists and once again began making appointments.

For rank insignia, Marine Warrant Officers wore the insignias of their respective departments until 1944 when they began wearing gold or silver bars broken by stripes of scarlet enamel. Army Warrant Officers got oval bars of gold and brown in 1942. Warrant Officers in the Army Air Forces wore oval bars of gold and light blue. In 1956 both changed to square-cornered gold or silver bars with blue enamel stripes for the Air Force and brown for the Army. There were four grades of Warrant Officers. The Warrant Officer (W-1) wore a gold bar with two enamel stripes, the Chief Warrant Officer (W-2) a gold bar with three stripes, the Chief Warrant Officer (W-3) a silver bar with two stripes and the Chief Warrant Officer (W-4) a silver bar with three stripes.

The Army found this system confusing so in 1969 asked its Institute of Heraldry to design another device. That was the silver bar with black enamel squares introduced in 1972 and still worn by Army Warrant Officers. Now the Warrant Officer (W-1) has one square and each higher grade gets another square up to Chief Warrant Officer (W-4) with four.

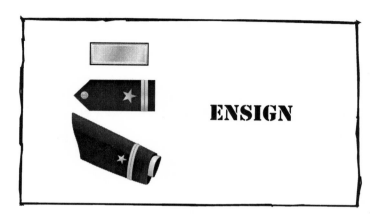

ENSIGN

Ensign comes from the Latin word *insignia* that meant, and still means, emblem or banner.

A warrior who carried his lord's banner or ensign became known as an ensign bearer and then just an Ensign. Later, the Ensign, still bearing his banner, led a military unit of about 500 foot soldiers called an *"ensigne."* As a military rank Ensign started in the French army as a junior officer and soon entered the French navy whose lowest commissioned rank is still *Enseigne.*

Ensigns served in our Revolutionary War in infantry regiments where they were the lowest ranking commissioned officers. After the war they also served in Regular Army infantry regiments from 1796 to 1814.

Ensigns did not join our Navy until 1862 when they needed a way to recognize graduates of the Naval Academy, who had been called Passed Midshipmen, and to have an equivalent rank to the Army Second Lieutenant. Also, in 1862, Ensigns wore a sleeve stripe of one one-quarter-inch wide gold lace, which increased to the present one-half-inch wide lace in 1881. The Ensign got his single gold bar rank insignia in 1922.

LIEUTENANT

A Lieutenant often takes the place of a superior officer when that officer is absent. The word comes from the French *lieu* (place) and *tenant* (holder). The Lieutenant then is one who holds the place of another. Since he took the place of a senior officer the Lieutenant ranked next to that person and was his deputy. Such was the case for Lieutenant General and Lieutenant Colonel, which I will discuss later.

The Navy Lieutenant Commander came about in a different way, which I will also discuss later. Those who served with Captains might have been called Lieutenant Captains but that title did not survive as a rank.

There may have been Lieutenants aboard British warships as early as the Twelfth Century when the ships carried groups of soldiers to do whatever fighting was necessary. A Captain commanded the soldiers and he might have had a Lieutenant. The rank appeared officially in the British navy about 1580 but soon disappeared. It became a designated rank in 1650 as the rank given to noblemen in training to become Captains. At that time there were no other ranks below

Captain so there could be three grades of Lieutenants on a ship—first, second and third.

The Lieutenant has been a part of our Navy since its beginning in 1775. In 1862 the Lieutenant's rank insignia was two gold bars. These became silver in 1877. In 1874 Lieutenants began wearing the sleeve stripes of two one-half-inch wide strips of gold lace.

The rank below Lieutenant in the early days of our Navy was Sailing Master, later Master, a Warrant Officer. After 1855 graduates of the Naval Academy filled those positions. Their complete title was "Master in line for Promotion" to distinguish them from the Warrant Masters who would not be promoted.

In 1883 the rank became Lieutenant, Junior Grade. In 1862 the Masters wore a gold bar for rank insignia, which became a silver bar in 1877. In 1881 they started wearing their current sleeve stripes of one one-half-inch and one one-quarter-inch wide strips of gold lace.

On land, there had been Lieutenants in the British and other armies for several centuries so it was logical to have the rank on duty in 1775 with our Army.

About 1832 First Lieutenants, except those in the Infantry, began wearing a bar—a gold one—on their shoulder straps as rank insignia. The bar had to be the same color as the borders of their shoulder straps, which were gold. Infantry First Lieutenants, however, wore shoulder straps with silver borders so their bars were of silver. After 1851 all Army officers wore shoulder straps with gold borders so the Infantry First Lieutenants then wore gold bars.

The situation was just the opposite when First Lieutenants wore their dress uniforms, which had gold epaulettes. Their rank insignia had to contrast with the gold so they wore silver bars. In 1872 the Army cleared up the confusion and made the bars on shoulder straps silver as well. Second Lieutenants did not have rank insignia but wore epaulettes or shoulder straps so their uniforms identified them as officers. When officers and enlisted men both started wearing khaki uniforms with plain shoulder straps during the Spanish-American War it became more difficult to recognize the Second Lieutenant. Other officers wore metal rank insignia on their shoulder straps or collars. In 1917 the Army settled that problem by making the gold bar the Second Lieutenant's badge of rank.

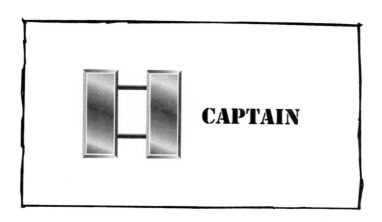

CAPTAIN

A Captain is a chieftain or head of a unit. The title comes from the Latin word *capitaneus* that meant chieftain, which in turn came from an older Latin word *caput* that meant head.

It would seem that a Captain could head a unit of any size but as armies evolved his post came to be at the head of a company, which by the Sixteenth Century was usually 100 to 200 men. That seemed to be the maximum number that one man could effectively manage in battle.

There appear to have been Captains leading Italian soldiers in the Tenth Century. In the Eleventh or Twelfth Century, British warships carried groups of soldiers commanded by Captains to do the fighting. The Navy's rank of Captain came from that practice, which I will describe later in the section on the Navy Captain.

Captains were company commanders in the British, French and other armies for centuries. They carried on that job in our Army and Marine Corps from 1775 to the present.

WHY IS A COLONEL CALLED A "KERNAL"?

In the Air Force, some Captains command some squadrons, which are about the equivalent of companies.

Army Captains got their rank insignia of two bars in about 1832 at the same time the First Lieutenants got one bar. The bars were gold except for the Infantry officers who wore silver bars until 1851. The two bars originated a few years earlier when Captains and Lieutenants both wore plain epaulettes whose differences were mostly in the size of the fringes. To help distinguish between the two ranks, Captains wore two strips or "holders" of gold or silver lace across the epaulette straps while Lieutenants wore one strip.

In 1872 Captains changed to silver bars. These were two separate bars embroidered onto shoulder straps or epaulettes. The "railroad tracks" used by Captains today appeared when officers started using metal pin-on rank insignia on their khaki or olive drab uniforms during or shortly after the Spanish-American War.

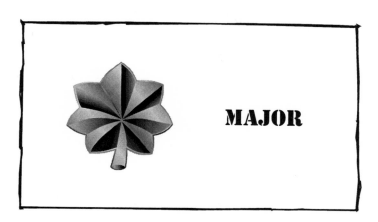

MAJOR

Major is a Latin word that means "greater" as compared to minor that means "less."

As a military rank it started out in the Sixteenth Century or earlier as Sergeant Major, who was the "greater" of the Sergeants. We could also think of the Sergeant Major as the "big" or "top" Sergeant but in those days he was an officer, the second or third in command of a regiment or similar unit.

The French started forming regiments in the Seventeenth Century by copying the Spanish technique of combining several companies into a column led by a Colonel. I will discuss the Colonel later. Sometimes the Captains of the companies making up the regiment would choose one of themselves as Colonel, another as Lieutenant Colonel and a third as Sergeant Major. Each would still be Captain of his own company.

In practice the Colonel was often absent looking after his interests at court or playing politics for his own and his regiment's benefit, leaving the Lieutenant Colonel as the effective commander of the regiment. He was usually aided by the Sergeant Major who was senior to the other Captains.

An important part of the Sergeant Major's job was forming the companies into a regimental unit and keeping them in proper formation during a battle or on the march. A loud, commanding voice was the key to that task and one of the major qualifications for the post—which goes to prove that some things never change.

As the regimental system became permanent during the Seventeenth and Eighteenth Centuries the Sergeant portion of the title gave way leaving just Major as the regiment's staff officer. Perhaps the other Captains objected to having a "big" Sergeant above them and other Sergeants below them. The title of Sergeant Major remained but as the top Sergeant among the common soldiers as he or she is today, although any good officer will admit that an effective Sergeant Major is still third in command of his regiment or other unit.

Majors in our Army started wearing oak leaves as rank insignia on their shoulder straps about 1832. Why the Army chose oak leaves remains a mystery. Navy and some Army officers had been wearing gold braid featuring oak leaves and acorns on their uniforms for several years. Generals, Admirals and some other senior officers still wear braid on their caps.

One story has it that the Navy chose oak leaf braid as a tribute to the oak lumber used to build its ships. While that is a good story it ignores the fact that some British and French officers also wore braid with oak leaves and still do today.

The British might have gotten the idea from the Germans who wore oak leaves in their headgear after a battle. That practice seems to go back a long time, perhaps to pagan warriors wearing the leaves as a tribute to whatever gods they worshiped. When the Elector of Hanover became King George I of Great Britain in 1714, his German followers might have introduced the oak leaf to the British military.

Another story traces the British use of oak leaves to King Charles II who escaped from his enemies in 1650 by hiding in an oak tree.

In any event, in 1832 the color of the leaves had to be opposite the color of the shoulder strap borders so Infantry Majors wore gold leaves while other Majors wore silver. After 1851 all Majors wore gold oak leaves. They did not have oak leaves on their epaulettes because the size of the fringes on their epaulettes and other features of their uniforms identified them as Majors.

LIEUTENANT COMMANDER

The Lieutenant Commander rank is one instance where our Navy did not adopt something from the British navy.

Shortly after 1775 a senior Lieutenant who was "Captain" of a smaller, 10- to 20-gun warship was called a Lieutenant Commanding, sometimes Lieutenant Commandant. In 1862 that rank became Lieutenant Commander. The British used the rank Senior Lieutenant until 1914 when they changed it to Lieutenant Commander.

These officers in our Navy began wearing embroidered gold oak leaves on their shoulder straps in 1862 and the two and one-half stripes of gold lace on their sleeve cuffs in 1874.

COMMANDER

A Commander is one who gives commands or has command over others. The word "command" comes from the Latin *mandare* that meant to give into one's hand, that is, put somebody in charge of something so he could command it.

As a rank, Commander appeared in the British navy about 1674 as "Master and Commander" to designate the officer under the Captain who was in charge of sailing a ship. He might also be second in command. The position had also been called sub-captain, under-captain, rector and master-commanding.

The Master and Commander could also command a smaller warship in which case he would be addressed as "Captain." Since every warship had a Captain, the British worked out a three grade system, depending on the size of ship commanded.

The Master and Commander became the lowest of the three grades. In 1794 the British cleared up the confusion a bit by shortening the title to just Commander. Our Navy took a different route but reached the same point a few years later. The second of the three grades of Captain was Master Commandant, which in 1838 became Commander. The third or lowest grade of Captain was "Lieutenant Commanding" which, as we have already seen, became Lieutenant Commander in 1862.

In 1862 Commanders began wearing embroidered silver oak leaves as rank insignia. They wore the leaves along with fouled anchors on their shoulder straps and epaulettes. In 1869 the Commander became a "three-striper" when he started wearing three one-half-inch wide stripes of gold lace on his sleeve cuffs.

COLONEL AND LIEUTENANT COLONEL

Colonels and Lieutenant Colonels owe their titles to the Sixteenth Century Spanish King Ferdinand. About 1505 he reorganized part of his army into twenty units called *colunelas* or columns. These consisted of about 1000 to 1250 men further organized into companies. The commander was the *cabo de colunela*, head of the column, or Colonel. Since the *colunelas* were royal or "crown" units they were also called *coronelias* and their commanders *coronels*.

Later in the Sixteenth Century the French copied the *colunela* idea and, in the Seventeenth Century, developed their regiments. They kept the title of Colonel and pronounced it the way it looks. The British copied the regiment organization from the French. They also borrowed the Colonel from the French but adopted the Spanish pronunciation of coronel. Why they did is a mystery. The British modified the pronunciation of coronet to "kernal" during several decades of use.

In the French and British armies the Colonels were usually noblemen whose other interests during peacetime or between battles kept them away from their regiments. Also., they had little taste for the mundane activities of drilling, training and marching. The Colonel's assistants—their lieutenants—took over at such times and any other times the Colonels were gone. The Colonel's lieutenants, of course, soon became the Lieutenant Colonels.

Colonels and Lieutenant Colonels led regiments throughout the Seventeenth Century and later, and were the obvious ranks for such positions when our Army started in 1775.

Colonels started wearing spread eagles as rank insignia in 1829 when they transferred the gold or gilt eagles that decorated their hat cockades to their collars. Eagles have been popular symbols in our and other military services at least as far back as the Romans. After 1831 most of the Colonels wore silver eagles on their gold epaulettes or gold-bordered shoulder straps. Infantry Colonels were the exceptions. They still wore the gold eagles to contrast with their silver epaulettes and silver-bordered shoulder straps until 1851 when they changed to gold epaulettes and shoulder straps with silver eagles.

Lieutenant Colonels started wearing oak leaves about 1832 on their shoulder straps. The leaves had to be the same color as the shoulder strap borders so Infantry Lieutenant Colonels wore silver leaves while others wore gold. This arrangement, not surprisingly, lead to confusion with some Majors and Lieutenant Colonels wearing gold leaves while others wore silver leaves. The Army did away with that bit of confusion in 1851 by having all officers wear straps with gold borders, all Majors wear gold oak leaves, and all Lieutenant Colonels wear silver leaves as they do today.

NAVY CAPTAIN

Captains entered the English navy in the Eleventh Century as the commanders of soldiers serving on ships to do the fighting when needed. The ships were commanded by Masters, who were Warrant Officers. The Masters were in charge of operating the ships while the Captains just concerned themselves with combat.

In the Fifteenth Century the Captains and their Lieutenants began taking over the executive functions on the ships. By 1747 the officers had full command of the ships so the British made Captain an official naval title and thereafter called the commander of any ship a Captain.

In 1748 the British navy established three grades of Captain, depending on the size of ship commanded. The top grade of Post-Captain was equal in rank to an Army Colonel. The two lower grades eventually became the ranks of Commander and Lieutenant Commander in the British navy.

Captain was the highest rank in our Navy from its beginning in 1775 until 1857 when Congress created the temporary rank of Flag Officer, which gave way to Commodore and

Rear Admiral in 1862. The commander of any warship was a Captain.

This situation lead to three grades of Captain ranking, according to the officer's duties, with an Army Brigadier General, Colonel or Lieutenant Colonel. The top grade of Captain became Commodore or Rear Admiral in 1862 while the lowest grade became Master Commandant in 1806 and Commander in 1837. The Navy Captain thus remained equal in rank to an Army Colonel.

The eagle as a rank insignia for Captain first appeared in 1852 when he wore an eagle perched on an anchor on his epaulettes and shoulder straps. On the epaulettes he also wore a silver star, which he lost to the Commodore in 1862.

The four sleeve stripes appeared in 1869. The four stripes also showed up on the Captain's shoulder marks in 1899. In 1941 he began wearing metal pin-on rank insignia on his khaki shirts. For that insignia he exchanged his eagle perched on an anchor for the spread-eagle worn by Army and Marine Colonels.

COMMODORE

The Dutch invented the Commodore rank about 1652 during one of their naval wars with England.

They found they needed officers to command squadrons but did not want to create more Admirals, perhaps to avoid paying Admirals' salaries. A Commodore's pay was only about half that of an Admiral.

The word comes from *comendador*, which means "having command over others" and might be of French or Spanish origin.

The Dutch leader William of Orange introduced the rank to the British navy after he became King William III of England in 1689. Sometime later the British merchant marine began calling the senior officer of a merchant fleet Commodore. The Dutch also used the broad command pennant, a wide swallow-tailed pennant, that has become identified with Commodores in many navies, merchant fleets and yacht clubs.

Our Navy used Commodore as an honorary title from the Revolutionary War to the Civil War for Captains commanding two or more ships operating together or had other significant additional responsibilities.

In 1862 Commodore became an official rank and the Navy promoted 18 Captains. They wore the single star on their epaulettes. In 1866 they began wearing the two-inch stripe on their sleeve cuffs. The broad stripe was inspired by the Commodore's broad pennant and, in effect, transferred it from his ship's masthead to his sleeve, a practice also adopted by many other navies and yacht clubs.

Commodore was a command rank in our Navy from 1862 to 1899. After that it was a rank to which Captains who had served in the Civil War were retired. The rank was reestablished on 9 April 1943 for World War II service, and 147 officers held it as a temporary rank. After the war the flag rank structure reverted to its prewar form. By 1 January 1950, no commodores remained on active duty.

When the Defense Officer Personnel Management Act (DOPMA) became law in 1982, O-7 officers were designated commodore admirals. The Navy selected 38 Captains to wear the broad stripe and single star. In 1983 the Defense Authorization bill changed the title to commodore. With President Reagan's signature on the Fiscal year 1986 Defense Authorization bill, O-7 officer were again called rear admiral (lower half).

ADMIRAL

Admiral comes from the Arabic term *amir-al-bahr* meaning commander of the seas.

Crusaders learned the term during their encounters with the Arabs, perhaps as early as the Eleventh Century. The Sicilians and later Genoese took the first two parts of the term and used them as one word, *amiral*. The French and Spanish gave their sea commanders similar titles. As the word was used by people speaking Latin or Latin-based languages it gained the "d" and endured a series of different endings and spellings leading to the English spelling "admyrall" in the Fourteenth Century and to "admiral" by the Sixteenth Century.

King Edward I appointed the first English Admiral in 1297 when he named William de Leyburn "Admiral of the Sea of the King of England." Sometime later the title became Lord High Admiral and appeared to be concerned with administering naval affairs rather than commanding at sea.

Admirals did become sea commanders by the Sixteenth or Seventeenth Century. When he commanded, the fleet the

Admiral would either be in the lead or the middle portion of the fleet. When the Admiral commanded from the middle portion of the fleet his deputy, the Vice Admiral, would be in the leading portion or van. The "vice" in Vice Admiral is a Latin word meaning deputy or one who acts in the place of another. The Vice Admiral is the Admiral's deputy or lieutenant and serves in the Admiral's place when he is absent. The British Vice Admiral also had a deputy. His post was at the rear of the fleet so instead of calling him the "Vice-Vice Admiral" his title became Rear Admiral. He was the "least important" of the flag officers so he commanded the reserves and the rear portion of the fleet. Sometimes he was called "Admiral in the rear." The British have had Vice and Rear Admirals since at least the Sixteenth Century.

Our Navy did not have any Admirals until 1862 because many people felt the title too reminiscent of royalty to be used in the republic's navy. Others saw the need for ranks above Captain.

Among them was John Paul Jones who pointed out that the Navy had to have officers who "ranked" with Army Generals. He also felt there must be ranks above Captain to avoid disputes among senior Captains. The various secretaries of the Navy repeatedly recommended to Congress that Admiral ranks be created because the other navies of the world used them and American senior officers were "often subjected to serious difficulties and embarrassments in the interchange of civilities with those of other nations."

Congress finally authorized nine Rear Admirals on July 16, 1862, although that was probably more for the needs of the rapidly expanding Navy during the Civil War than any international considerations.

Two years later Congress authorized the appointment of a Vice Admiral from among the nine Rear Admirals. That was David Glasgow Farragut. Another bill allowed the President to appoint Farragut Admiral on July 25, 1866, and David Dixon Porter became Vice Admiral.

When Farragut died in 1870 Porter became Admiral and Stephen C. Rowan Vice Admiral. When they died Congress did not allow the promotion of any of the Rear Admirals to succeed them so there were no more Admirals or Vice Admirals by promotion until 1915 when Congress authorized an Admiral and a Vice Admiral each for the Atlantic, Pacific and Asiatic fleets.

There was one Admiral in the interim, however.

In 1899 Congress recognized George Dewey's accomplishments during the Spanish-American War by authorizing the President to appoint him Admiral of the Navy. He held that rank until he died in 1917. Nobody has since held that title. In 1944 Congress approved the five-star Fleet Admiral rank. The first to hold it were Ernest J. King, William D. Leahy and Chester W. Nimitz. The Senate confirmed their appointments December 15, 1944. The fourth Fleet Admiral, William H. Halsey, got his fifth star in December 1945. None have been appointed since.

The sleeve stripes now used by Admirals and Vice Admirals date from March 11, 1869, when the Secretary of the Navy's General Order Number 90 specified that for their "undress" uniforms Admirals would wear a two-inch stripe with three half-inch stripes above it and Vice Admirals the two-inch stripe with two half-inch stripes above it. The Rear Admiral got his two-inch stripe and one half-inch stripe in 1866.

Previously the sleeve stripes were much more elaborate. When the Rear Admiral rank started in 1862 the sleeve arrangement was three stripes of three-quarter-inch lace alternating with three stripes of quarter-inch lace. It was some ten inches from top to bottom. The Vice Admiral, of course, had even more stripes and when Farragut became Admiral in 1866 he had so many stripes they reached from his cuffs almost to his elbow. On their dress uniforms the admirals wore bands of gold embroidery of live oak leaves and acorns.

WHY IS A COLONEL CALLED A "KERNAL"?

The admirals of the 1860s wore the same number of stars on their shoulders as admirals of corresponding grades do today. In 1899 the Navy's one Admiral (Dewey) and 18 Rear Admirals put on the new shoulder marks, as did the other officers when wearing their white uniforms, but kept their stars instead of repeating the sleeve cuff stripes.

GENERAL

A General usually has overall command of a whole army. His title comes from the Latin word *generalis* that meant something pertaining to a whole unit of anything rather than just to a part. As a military term General started as an adjective, as in Captain General indicating the Captain who had overall or "general" command of the army.

Before the Sixteenth Century armies were usually formed only when needed for a war or campaign. The king would be the commander but he might appoint a Captain General to command in his name. Later, when the title of Colonel became popular some kings called their commanders Colonel General. The British Army stopped using the Captain part of the title by the Eighteenth Century leaving just General as the top commander.

Some nations still use the Colonel General rank, among them the Soviet Union and East Germany. The king or his Captain General would often be away from the army since they had interests elsewhere, so the job of actually running the army fell to the Captain General's assistant—his lieutenant—the Lieutenant General. This was not a permanent rank until the Seventeenth Century. One of the Colonels might be appointed Lieutenant General for a particular campaign or war but he would still command his own regiment. Since he might also be Captain of a company in his regiment, it was possible for one man to serve as Captain, Colonel and General simultaneously.

The army's chief administrative officer was the Sergeant Major General who was also appointed for the particular campaign or war. He would be an experienced soldier, possibly a commoner, who served as chief of staff. For much of his administrative work he dealt with the regimental Sergeant Majors, thus his title meant "overall" or "chief" Sergeant Major. His duties included such things as supply, organization, and forming the army for battle or march. Here again, as with the regimental Sergeant Major, a loud, commanding voice was a key requirement.

As the General ranks became fixed during the Seventeenth Century the Sergeant portion fell away leaving the title as Major General. We can see this trend in England where in 1655 Oliver Cromwell, who ruled that nation temporarily as Lord Protector, organized the country into eleven military districts each commanded by a Major General.

The Lieutenant General and Sergeant Major General dealt directly with the Colonels who lead the regiments making up the army. When there got to be too many regiments for the two generals to handle effectively they organized battle groups or brigades, usually composed of three or more regiments. Brigade comes from the Florentine word *brigare* that in turn came from the Latin *briga*, both of which referred to fighting or strife. The brigade's commander was the Brigadier, who in some armies later became Brigadier General.

When our Army started in 1775 the Continental Congress commissioned George Washington General and Commander-in-Chief. He and his Major and Brigadier Generals wore various colored ribbons to show their ranks. There were no Lieutenant Generals in that army.

In June 1780 General Washington ordered the Major Generals to wear a uniform that included two gold epaulettes with two silver stars on each epaulette. Brigadier Generals were to wear gold epaulettes with one silver star on each. General Washington might have chosen the stars because the generals and admirals of the French forces serving in that war wore stars. Another story has it that he was inspired by the stars in our new flag. The General's stars, then, are the oldest rank insignia still in use by our armed forces.

General Washington was the first to wear three stars when he became the nation's first Lieutenant General in 1798. After he died in 1799 there was not another Lieutenant General until 1855. The three stars appeared again, however, by 1832 as the insignia of the Major General who commanded the Army.

In 1855 Congress honored Winfield Scott for his service as commanding general since 1841 and for his accomplishments in 1847 during the war with Mexico by making him a Brevet Lieutenant General. He held that rank until he retired in 1861.

The next Lieutenant General was Ulysses S. Grant in 1864. Two years later he became the first General of the Army of the United States and chose four stars as his rank insignia. When Grant became President in 1869 he appointed William T. Sherman General of the Army and Phillip H. Sheridan Lieutenant General. Sherman changed the rank insignia in 1872 to a gold embroidered coat of arms of the United States between two silver stars.

After Sherman retired in 1884 there was not supposed to be another General of the Army, but in 1888 Congress relented and permitted the President to promote Sheridan who died two months later. Congress allowed another Lieutenant General promotion in 1895, one in 1900, five between 1903 and 1906, two in 1918 during World War I, one in 1929 and then no more until 1939. Our Army has been supplied with Lieutenant Generals since, as has the Marine Corps since 1942 and the Air Force since 1947.

There were no more full Generals after Sheridan died in 1884 until 1917 when Tasker H. Bliss, the Army Chief of Staff, and John J. Pershing, the commander of the U.S. forces in France during World War I, went from Major General to General (emergency) so they could have ranks equal to the allied commanders with whom they dealt. They changed the rank insignia back to four stars. In 1918, Peyton C. March also became a General.

In 1919 Congress honored Pershing for his wartime service by permitting the President to promote him to General of the Armies of the United States, which he held until he retired in 1924. He chose his own insignia, which was four stars. Nobody else has received that rank during his lifetime.

In 1976 Congress authorized the President to posthumously appoint George Washington General of the Armies of the United States and specified that he would rank first among all officers of the Army, past or present.

Congress did not allow the promotion of any more full Generals from 1918 to 1929 when the Major General chosen to be Chief of Staff also became a General so he could have a rank equal to the Chief of Naval Operations. Promotions for other Generals did not come until World War II, with the exception of a permanent promotion to General for Generals Bliss and March in June 1930. The Army still has several Generals, the Marines have had at least one General since 1945 and the Air Force, which started with three in 1947, also has several.

During World War II our Army got so big that even full Generals were not enough so in 1944 Congress created the new rank of General of the Army and specified five stars as its insignia. Congress did not revive the General of the Army rank held by Grant, Sherman and Sheridan. The World War II Generals of the Army were in a separate category from the

Civil War Generals of the Army. In December 1944 the President appointed George C. Marshall, Douglas MacArthur, Dwight D. Eisenhower and Henry H. Arnold Generals of the Army. In 1949 Arnold's title became General of the Air Force. Omar N. Bradley got his fifth star in 1950.

As to the question of Pershing being a six-star general, there can be no answer unless Congress creates the General of the Armies rank again and specifies the insignia. Pershing does rank ahead of the Five-star Generals, he comes right after Washington, but he chose his own insignia and he never wore more than four stars.

APPENDIX I
CHART OF COMPARITIVE RANKS
ENLISTED

	Army	Navy Coast Guard	Marine Corps	Air Force
E-1	Private	Seaman Recruit	Private	Airman Basic
E-2	Private E-2	Seaman Apprentice	Private First Class	Airman
E-3	Private First Class	Seaman	Lance Corporal	Airman First Class
E-4	Corporal / Specialist	Petty Officer Third Class	Corporal	Senior Airman
E-5	Sergeant	Petty Officer Second Class	Sergeant	Staff Sergeant

E-6	Staff Sergeant	Petty Officer First Class	Staff Sergeant	Technical Sergeant
E-7	Sergeant First Class	Chief Petty Officer	Gunnery Sergeant	Master Sergeant
E-8	Master Sergeant / First Sergeant	Senior Chief Petty Officer	Master Sergeant / First Sergeant	Senior Master Sergeant
E-9	Sergeant Major / Command Sergeant Major	Master Chief Petty Officer	Master Gunnery Sergeant / Sergeant Major	Chief Master Sergeant

APPENDIX II
CHART OF COMPARITIVE RANKS
WARRANT OFFICER

	Army	Navy	Coast Guard	Marine Corps
W-1	Warrant Officer One	Warrant Officer One (Discontinued 1975)	Warrant Officer One N/A	Warrant Officer One (Gold)
W-2	Warrant Officer Two	Warrant Officer Two	Warrant Officer Two	Warrant Officer Two (Gold)
W-3	Warrant Officer Three	Warrant Officer Three	Warrant Officer Three	Warrant Officer Three (Silver)

	Army	Navy	Coast Guard	Marine Corps
W-4	Warrant Officer Four	Warrant Officer Four	Warrant Officer Four	Warrant Officer Four (Silver)
W-5	Warrant Officer Five	Warrant Officer Five Established 2002	Warrant Officer Five N/A	Warrant Officer Five

APPENDIX III
CHART OF COMPARITIVE RANKS
OFFICER

	Army	Navy Coast Guard	Marine Corps	Air Force
O-1	Second Lieutenant (Gold)	Ensign	Second Lieutenant (Gold)	Second Lieutenant (Gold)
O-2	First Lieutenant (Silver)	Lieutenant, Junior Grade	First Lieutenant (Silver)	First Lieutenant (Silver)
O-3	Captain (Silver)	Lieutenant	Captain (Silver)	Captain (Silver)
O-4	Major (Gold)	Lieutenant Commander	Major (Gold)	Major (Gold)

O5	Lieutenant Colonel (Silver)	Commander	Lieutenant Colonel (Silver)	Lieutenant Colonel (Silver)
O6	Colonel (Silver)	Captain	Colonel (Silver)	Colonel (Silver)
O7	Brigadier General	Rear Admiral (lower half)	Brigadier General	Brigadier General
O8	Major General	Rear Admiral (upper half)	Major General	Major General
O9	Lieutenant General	Vice Admiral	Lieutenant General	Lieutenant General
O10	General	Admiral	General	General

BIBLIOGRAPHY

Boatner, Mark. Military Customs and Traditions. Westport, Ct.: Greenwood Press, 1976.

Carman, W.Y. A Dictionary of Military Uniform. New York: Scribner's, 1977.

Castano, J.B. The Naval Officer's Uniform Guide. Annapolis, Md.: Naval Institute Press, 1975.

Elting, John R., ed. Military Uniforms in America. Vol. 2, Years of Growth, 1796-1851. San Rafael, Ca.: Presidio Press, 1977.

Dupuy, R. Ernest Dupuy and Trevor N. Dupuy. The Encyclopedia of Military History. New York: Harper & Row, 1977.

Finke, Detmar H. "Insignia of Rank in the Continental Army." Military Collector & Historian, Fall l956. This is the journal of the Company of Military Historians, must reading for anyone interested in uniforms or insignia.

Finke, Detmar H. and Mark Haynes, "U.S. Army Insignia of Rank." Fact sheet of the Army Center of Military History, 7 August 1973.

Gordon, Lawrence. Military Origins. New York: A.S. Barnes & Co., 1971.

Grosvenor, Gilbert. Insignia and Decorations of the U.S. Armed Forces. Washington, D.C.: National Geographic Society, 1943.

Kerrigan, Evans. American Badges and Insignia. New York: Viking Press, 1967.

Lovette, Leland P. Naval Customs, Traditions and Usage. Annapolis, Md.:Naval Institute Press, 1939.

Mack, William P. and Royal W. Connell. Naval Ceremonies, Customs and Traditions. Annapolis, Md.: Naval Institute Press, 1980.

Nalty, Bernard C. United States Marine Corps Ranks and Grades, 1775-1969. Washington, D.C.: Historical Division, Headquarters, U.S. Marine Corps, 1970.

Onions, C.T. The Oxford Dictionary of English Etymology. Oxford, Eng.: Clarendon Press, 1966.

Oxford English Dictionary: Compact Edition. Oxford, Eng.: Oxford University Press, 1971.

Partridge, Eric. Origins: A Short Entymological Dictionary of Modern English. New York: Macmillan, 1958.

Perrin, W.G. "Vice-Vice-Admiral and Rear-Admiral of the United Kingdom." Mariner's Mirror 14, no. 1 (Jan. 1928): 26-31.

Peterson, Mendel. "American Epaulettes, 1775-1820." Military Collector & Historian, June 1950 and March 1951.

Powell, Isabel. "The Early Naval Lieutenant." Mariner's Mirror, Dec. 1923.

Steffen, Randy. The Horse Soldier: The United States Cavalryman-His Uniforms, Arms, Accoutrements, and Equipments, 1776-1943. Norman: University of Oklahoma Press, 1977.

Tily, James C. The Uniforms of the United States Navy. New York: T. Yoseloff, 1964.

U.S. Army. Adjutant General's Office. "Fact Sheet, 24, Mar. 1955." Unpublished. A discussion of the ranks of General of the Armies and General of the Army.

U.S. Army. Office of the Chief of Military History. The American Soldier. Lithographs, 1964-1966.

United States Quartermaster Department. Uniforms of the Army of the United States (Illustrated) From 1774 to 1889, 1898 to 1907. Authorized by the Secretary of War and Prepared and Published by the Quartermaster General. American Lithographic Co., 1890-1909. Two volumes. Paintings by H.A. Ogden. Reprinted New York: T.Yoseloff, 1959.

U.S. Navy. Naval History Division. Uniforms of the United States Navy. Lithographs, 1966 and 1967.

Weekley, Ernest. An Etymological Dictionary of Modern English, London: J. Murray, 1921.

Weiner, Frederick. "Three Stars and Up." The Infantry Journal, June, July, September and October 1945.

Uniform regulations of the military services (title varies).

For the Finest in Nautical and Historical Fiction and Nonfiction

www.FireshipPress.com

Interesting • Informative • Authoritative

9 781934 757598